T0037094

BECAUSE
CLAUDETTE

Tracey Baptiste
illustrated by Tonya Engel

DIAL BOOKS FOR YOUNG READERS

COLORED
ATED IN REAR

Because fifteen-year-old Claudette Colvin didn't give up her seat on the bus for a white person on March 2, 1955, she was arrested.

Because she was arrested, her parents asked a lawyer named Fred Gray for help.

Mr. Gray wanted to know more about Claudette,
so he asked fellow activist Rosa Parks to meet with her.

Because Mrs. Parks was a member of the civil rights group the National Association for the Advancement of Colored People, or NAACP, she invited Claudette to one of their youth meetings. Claudette liked the meetings and kept going.

Some nights the meetings ran late. When that happened, Claudette stayed at Mrs. Parks' home.

Claudette chatted while Mrs. Parks sewed, and the two became friends.

This was a good thing, because Claudette's classmates were upset with her for causing trouble, and Claudette found herself more and more alone.

But Claudette wasn't alone. Because she had studied Sojourner Truth and Harriet Tubman and Frederick Douglass at school, she learned how they worked hard and caused trouble so Black people would be treated fairly.

That year, Aurelia Browder, Mary Louise Smith,
Susie McDonald, and Rosa Parks also caused trouble
when they said "no" to giving up their bus seats.

Because of them, Claudette truly wasn't alone.

People had enough of the unfair bus laws,
so many came to Montgomery, Alabama,
to talk about what they could do.
    Because the meetings were organized
by churches, many preachers came too.

One was a relatively unknown young preacher named Martin Luther King, Jr.

Because Dr. King was an electric speaker, he got people excited to take action.

They decided on a bus boycott. Professor Jo Ann Robinson was ready to organize it. A year before, she had tried and failed to get W. A. Gayle, the mayor of Montgomery, to change the bus law.

Because churches could pass out flyers on Sunday, the boycott was planned for Monday, December 5.

When the boycott began, many people needed
to travel far, so car rides were arranged.

Because there were not enough cars for everyone,
a lot of people walked.

As shoes got worn down, people all over the country
sent donations.

Because Mayor Gayle still refused to change
the law, Fred Gray challenged it in court.
Because Claudette was impressive and engaging,
Mr. Gray asked her to be the final witness on the stand.

Claudette was so convincing,
the judges ordered a change
to the bus law.

When the city and the state refused to follow the court's
orders, the boycott went on . . . for many more months.

E·UNDER·LAW·I

The case then went to the Alabama
Supreme Court. Those judges agreed
the bus laws needed to be changed.
Mayor Gayle challenged the ruling again,
but the court forced him to comply.

Because of that, on December 20,
1956, the bus boycott ended.

Claudette learned about this like most other people . . . from reading the morning newspaper.

BAMA JOURNAL

CATION IS KNOCKED OUT

On December 21, 1956, anyone could sit
wherever they liked on the bus.

And all of it happened
because of Claudette.

AUTHOR'S NOTE

The idea for *Because Claudette* came from an event to honor Ms. Claudette Colvin in 2019. She had retired and was moving from New York back to Alabama. Fred Gray, her lawyer, spoke about her influence on the Montgomery boycott, saying it might never have happened if it weren't for Claudette. I immediately thought about the many small acts of resistance that often lead to a bigger movement.

There are many other acts of resistance that contributed to the Montgomery boycott. The first Black-led bus boycott happened in Baton Rouge, Louisiana, two years before. There were other individuals like Sarah Mae Flemming, who also refused to give up her bus seat in Columbia, South Carolina, on June 22, 1954, the year before Claudette did the same.

Movements are made of small individual acts that come together into something bigger. No act of resistance stands alone, and each one matters, no matter how small.

FOR FURTHER READING

BOOKS:

Claudette Colvin Refuses to Move: Courageous Kid of the Civil Rights Movement by Ebony Joy Wilkins, illustrated by Mark Simmons

She Persisted: Claudette Colvin by Lesa Cline-Ransome, illustrated by Gillian Flint

INTERNET:

Claudette Colvin
https://kids.britannica.com/kids/article/Claudette-Colvin/544733

Claudette Colvin
https://www.biography.com/activist/claudette-colvin

Claudette Colvin: the woman who refused to give up her bus seat—nine months before Rosa Parks
https://www.theguardian.com/society/2021/feb/25/claudette-colvin-the-woman-who-refused-to-give-up
-her-bus-seat-nine-months-before-rosa-parks

This one goes to Norah
—T.B.

*To my mother and all who endured and
pushed for freedom from segregation
and Jim Crow laws in the South.
Thank you for your sacrifices, love, and dedication.*
—T.E.

DIAL BOOKS FOR YOUNG READERS
An imprint of Penguin Random House LLC, New York

First published in the United States of America by Dial Books for Young Readers, an imprint of Penguin Random House LLC, 2022

Text copyright © 2022 by Tracey Baptiste • Illustrations copyright © 2022 by Tonya Engel

Penguin supports copyright. Copyright fuels creativity, encourages diverse voices, promotes free speech, and creates a vibrant culture. Thank you for buying an authorized edition of this book and for complying with copyright laws by not reproducing, scanning, or distributing any part of it in any form without permission. You are supporting writers and allowing Penguin to continue to publish books for every reader.

Dial & colophon are registered trademarks of Penguin Random House LLC. • Visit us online at penguinrandomhouse.com.
Library of Congress Cataloging-in-Publication Data is available.

Manufactured in China • ISBN 9780593326404
3 5 7 9 10 8 6 4 2
TOPL

Design by Jason Henry • Text set in Avenir • The artwork for this book was created with acrylic underpainting and oils on textured vellum paper.
The publisher does not have any control over and does not assume any responsibility for author or third-party websites or their content.